Lilith

The Dark Goddess of Divine Feminine Energy

Preface

Dare to awaken the Lilith within! Step into a journey of spiritual awakening and living your truth.

Have you ever wondered what freedom lies within the darkest parts of ourselves?

Do you ever feel like your power and passion have been taken from you, and you need to rediscover them?

Did you ever think about taking control of your life and challenging the norms?

Whether you're looking to challenge patriarchal norms, spark creativity, or embark on a journey of personal healing, this book is your roadmap, and Lilith will be your fierce guide.

If self-discovery and actualization are fulfilments you strive for, do not hesitate to use this book as either a starting point or another step along the way.

Table of Contents

Introduction

"In the long fifty-year night,

these are the words that crawl out of the wall:

Suffer. Monster. Burn in Hell.

When morning comes,

I will finally tell.

Amen."

—Carol Ann Duffy, *The World's Wife*, "The Devil's Wife - 4. Night"

Have you ever felt a quiet, unshakable force within you —one that refuses to conform, that craves freedom and passion?

Many people, especially women, have felt this way before. There is a comfort in knowing that others have experienced what you have and even attributed it to an energy beyond their existence. It is possible that the spirit of Lilith, the Dark Goddess of the Divine Feminine, is speaking to you and through you. Perhaps it is time to listen to what she says.

But who is Lilith?

From possible Sumerian wild spirit to Biblical demoness to medieval seductress, Lilith is a figure steeped in myth from what seems to be the very beginnings of time. Lilith —Goddess, Seductress, Hag, Serpent, Black Moon, Queen of Hell, Mother of Demons, Rebel, Protector of Women— she has been known by many and throughout time as a woman of much versatility and interpretations. Her most famous iteration is that of the First Woman, Adam's first wife, created of the same earth and who refused to lie beneath him. But that is just one facet of her many characteristics.

And just like most women, she became misunderstood and, in her defiance, feared and abhorred. Not anymore. Lilith has been reborn as a symbol of the untamed feminine, rebellion, and self-discovery. Through her, we invite you to join us on a story exploring the deeper sides of this mysterious and powerful woman.

In these pages, Lilith will slowly be demystified and presented as a relatable and transformative archetype in which all women can see a part of themselves. Through this engagement with her energy, it becomes inevitable that one can be inspired to strive toward personal growth, empowerment, and spiritual awakening.

Whether you have never heard or thought of Lilith before, or if the Dark Goddess has always been a fixture in your life, this book will carve a space for you in our collective transformation. This is a comprehensive guide, blending Lilith's form in historical context, psychological insights, and spiritual practice, ensuring an inclusive and holistic approach. It is not just about the theorctical or the abstract; we understand that practical guidance and focus are needed to understand and harness this profound spirit. Here, you will find hands-on methods, rituals, and exercises that help you connect with Lilith's energy.

This book truly is a journey, following a map to the inner parts of yourself. Together, we will understand the myths and history that shaped Lilith through different eras. Then, we will understand our inner psyche and turmoil, accepting her role as a shadow self and a guide to facing our fears, as well as her symbolism in the celebration of sexual sovereignty and self-expression. We will delve deeper into our current time period and explore her influence on modern feminism and spiritual movements. Finally, you will gain practical steps to integrate Lilith's energy into your daily life.

No matter who you are or where you are on your journey of self-discovery, Lilith's story can resonate with your struggles and desires. Know that you, too, can harness the transformative power of Lilith and live a more empowered life.

So, are you ready to walk alongside Lilith and uncover the divine feminine power within?

Then, let us begin.

Chapter 1

Lilith in Myth and History

The outside world has always perceived women as straddling a line between two extremes: the tempting vixen and the pure angel, the homewrecker, and the mother, the damsel in distress, and the madwoman in the attic. They have never been allowed to exist in the in-between, the moderate, the ordinary. And it should come as no surprise that the First Woman is awarded such treatment as well.

A figure with roots in mythology, religion, and occult traditions, Lilith embodies women's permanent position, stretched between two polarities. She is an enigma. She is equal parts divine and demonic. And just like any woman, she is one whose story has been told over and over again by men who villainized her, casting her away as the root of all (their) evil.

But who, truly, is Lilith? How has this figure evolved across cultures and time?

The Mysterious Origins of Lilith

Sumerian and Babylonian Mythology

From the cradle of civilization in Ancient Mesopotamia, we find the first theorized mentions of this immortal figure. While Lilith herself is not explicitly mentioned by name in Sumerian and Babylonian texts, it is striking how similar she appears to be to several figures and concepts in their mythology. We begin with her very name, which some etymologists argue originates from the Akkadian language of Babylonia, with the terms *lili* and *lilītu*. These were storm demons, spirits of chaos, generally attributed to female characteristics. They were believed to roam the wilderness, carried through strong winds, causing harm. Many academics have also found evidence of her presence in the famous Sumerian *Epic of Gilgamesh*, where a malicious creature or spirit fearfully flees from the hero after he slays her snake and bird companions.

There has always been more to Lilith than what meets the eye. Amulets uncovered archaeologically, known as the Arslan Tash amulets, have shown that the name Lilith has existed for centuries beyond our common era. She has been compared and connected with many other Sumerian and Babylonian goddesses and demons. From the Mesopotamian demoness Lamashtu, who kidnapped breastfeeding children, to the Sumerian goddess Inanna of love, war, and fertility, Lilith's character has always been one of speculation and mystery. Some scholars ponder if she could represent a darker counterpart to the benevolent goddesses, emphasizing her connection to *lilitu* and their eerie predatory nature.

In all these theories, stories, and myths, one thing becomes clear. Lilith emerged as a symbol of a dangerous, untamed force connected to female fertility, death, and sexuality through Babylonian lore. She is feared, yes, but there is also a measure of respect as she embodies a dual aspect of destroyer and protector.

Jewish Folklore: *The Alphabet of Ben Sira*

There are many texts and accounts in Jewish traditions that are believed to have referenced Lilith in a direct or indirect way. However, the clearest account of the story of Lilith in Jewish thought is *The Alphabet of Ben Sira*. Here, we have the oldest known record of Lilith as Adam's first wife and the subsequent rebellion that followed.

The story follows that after God created Adam, he did not want Adam to be alone, and so formed Lilith from the same clay from which he made Adam. Afterwards, they began to fight as Lilith refused to lie beneath him, arguing that since both were created from the earth, they were equal. Adam refused, claiming to be superior and that he must lie on top of her. When it was evident neither would listen to the other, Lilith ran away from Adam, who turned to God for assistance.

Immediately, God sent three angels, Senoy, Sansenoy, and Semangelof, to retrieve her. They caught her in the midst of the sea, where they warned her that if she did not return, she would be cursed to have one hundred of her children die every day, and she would be drowned in the sea. In retaliation, she vowed that she would be a harbinger of death and disease to newborns —as such, in many Jewish traditions, women in labor and infants still wear an amulet inscribed with the names of the three angels as protection against Lilith.

Thus, Adam's first wife —she who rejected subservience to him and asserted her equal status and independence— was hunted down and shunned. It's vital to note that the pivotal moment in this story is her autonomy and taking charge of her own life. She did not wait for anyone to help her out of the unfairness she found herself in; her defiance was shown in her self-imposed exile, refusing to bow down to offers or threats. And for leaving Eden for freedom over subjugation, she became demonized as a seductress and child-stealer in subsequent early Jewish texts. For her rebellion, autonomy, and challenge to patriarchal authority, she was portrayed as a warning against disobedience.

Medieval Mysticism

In the medieval world, the figure of Lilith continued to grow into a multifaceted but feared figure, with emphasis on her existence as a warning and forbearance to women against rebellion. In Kabbalistic traditions (a school of thought in Jewish mysticism), they attempted to establish a more exact relationship between Lilith and God, her creation ranging from a soul that emerged from the Great Abyss, or from the realm of evil, or from the darkness that surrounded the "first light." Ultimately, her role in most Kabbalistic texts was as a dark, shadowy counterpart to the divine feminine. She became one of the Dark Goddesses, Queen of the *Sitra Ahra* ("Other Side"), seen as the Serpent who tempts men with knowledge.

Through art and poetry, Lilith blended elements of beauty, danger, seduction, and rebellion. Her depictions were shaped by the preexisting Jewish folklore, a growing Christian demonology, and the evolving cultural perceptions of femininity and sin. In art, Lilith is sometimes illustrated with a woman's upper body and a serpent's lower body, inspired by her association with the serpent in the Garden of Eden. She is also often shown as a demonic figure with wings, birdlike claws, and wild hair. These portrayals emphasized her hybrid nature as a beast and woman, a dangerous supernatural being. In line with her association with the night, she was occasionally drawn alongside nocturnal animals like owls or bats, adding to her otherworldly nature.

Of course, medieval manuscripts also had a habit of portraying Lilith as a beautiful, seductive woman, reinforcing her role as a tempter and corruptor of men. In many texts where she was linked to sin, lust, and death, Lilith embodied the dangers of unchecked desire and rebellion against divine order. Her irresistible beauty brought doom to those who succumbed to her charms, and she became a cautionary tale against female rebellion, symbolizing the dangers of straying from religious and social expectations.

It is a strange thing, her duality. She is a figure of both fascination and fear, almost as though men cannot decide if they love or hate the temptation, the hidden knowledge, the forbidden fruit. Her character as being alluring yet malevolent helped reinforce her fearsome reputation, ensuring men could use her as a warning, and women could take her as a premonition.

These medieval descriptions will still resonate with women today. As men are paraded as the helpless victims of her wiles and Lilith is branded a seductress who preys on men, women are reminded of the pressures they feel to conform to a society that wants them as neither prudes nor sluts. You come to realize that Lilith is just like you—another woman who found herself on the end of a man's accusatory finger.

Lilith's Evolution in Modern Literature and Culture

Despite her rare presence in mainstream medieval Christian art, the figure of Lilith in mystical, Jewish, and esoteric traditions heavily influenced later Renaissance and Romantic depictions of her that carried forward into the modern era. One of her earliest appearances in literature was in Goethe's *Faust: The First Part of the Tragedy,* where she is introduced by the demon, Mephistopheles, and dances with Faust. Again, the depiction emphasized her nature as a danger to man through her irresistible beauty,

One of the most famous depictions of Lilith from the 19th century is Dante Gabriel Rossetti's painting of *Lady Lilith*. In it, she is depicted as a beautiful, long-haired woman, surrounded by poppies (symbols of death and cold) and white roses (symbols of sterile passion), and gazing into a mirror. Rossetti wrote a sonnet to accompany this piece that truly summarized the cultural perceptions of Lilith and the way female autonomy and sexuality were demonized.

It is fascinating how, when they wanted to depict her in an abhorrent image, all they did was place a mirror in her hand, allowing her beauty to belong to herself and her own gaze, instead of a man's, and called in self-absorption.

Male poets and writers continued to attribute to her all the fantasies they dreamt of —loving Adam despite his mistreatment, prostrating herself as a slave to Adam, finding salvation through a man— never allowing her a moment's rest. Well into the 21st century, men continue this fetishization of Lilith through poetry, novels, plays, films, TV shows, and video games, emphasizing her demonic origins, her monstrous nature, and her seductive dangers.

It was only with her adoption by second-wave feminists that Lilith became an icon of liberation, a symbol of feminist defiance, and a beacon of sexual freedom. Feminists reclaimed her story from mythology and religious texts, transforming her from a demonized figure into a representation of women's resistance to the patriarchy. Feminists used her image to challenge the "Eve Ideal," where women are expected to be submissive and obedient, bearing the brunt of men's blame. Also, in alignment with second-wave feminism's focus on sexual liberation, breaking taboos, and particularly destigmatizing female sexuality, Lilith's portrayal as a sensual figure helped bolster their ideals.

One of the clearest examples of Lilith's feminist adoption is *Lilith Magazine*, founded in 1976, which aimed to amplify women's voices. She continued to inspire popular culture and media in Adrienne Rich's poetry, Judy Chicago's art, the all-women music festival Lilith Fair, Octavia Butler's novels, and, of course, Judith Plaskow's famous midrash, *The Coming of Lilith*. For the first time, Eve and Lilith reconcile, a sisterhood is formed where women do not compete for a man's attention and realize that female solidarity is the way forward for us all. She has become a complex figure of defiance and empowerment, allowing Lilith to inspire activism and cultural expression.

Over time, Lilith has transformed from demon to archetype, whether it be the female seductress or protector. Her story in every age reflects the broader cultural anxieties that exist surrounding female independence and sexuality. Her adaptability is her appeal, as she becomes the symbol for several movements, from religious fear to neopagan and occult worship, to feminist empowerment. She resonates across time and culture as a woman breaking free of her restraints, a woman misunderstood and blamed, and a woman who defies expectations.

Her energy lives within us all. As the spirit of Lilith is ingrained in our practices and lives, her role as the shadow-self archetype shines through.

So, take a minute and wonder, how does Lilith challenge your perception of power, freedom, and femininity?

What does Lilith's story mean to you?

Chapter 2

Lilith as the Shadow Self

What parts of yourself have you been taught to hide? Your anger, your wild desires, your hunger for freedom?

We have seen how Lilith was demonized by religion, myth, and men for sharing these same qualities that all women possess. The most basic rights of what it means to be human have been denied to women for too long as they are asked and forced to repress the natural parts of who they are. Here, we will introduce Lilith as the embodiment of the shadow feminine—the raw, untamed aspects of ourselves that society rejects.

There is always a misconception and stigma associated with shadows and the dark. From our childhoods, we believe that the dark is a thing to fear, that it symbolizes a frightening and unknown void that cannot be touched or controlled. We are taught that shadows are the imprints of who we are when we are devoid of light. But more often than not, shadows and darkness carry something invaluable to life—freedom. When no one sees you, that is when you possess the power to be anything and everything your mind can conjure, let your heart's true desires run wild. In the dark, through our shadows, we are real. And that is what we must understand: that through Lilith's energy, we will find the strength and the endurance to embrace our shadow self.

Understanding the Shadow Self

What is the shadow self? In analytical psychology, the shadow is an unconscious aspect of the personality that contains all the things about ourselves that we repress, whether it's because they are evil, socially unacceptable, harmful to others, or detrimental to our own health. One of the ways the shadow may be personified is through archetypes that relate to the collective unconscious, the shared mental concepts of the world. Carl Jung championed the idea of the shadow in his model of the human psyche, recognizing the deep complexity of our internal world.

Jung was fascinated by the shadow as "the thing a person has no wish to be," especially as he believed that failure to recognize and reconcile with our shadow elements often led to our problems within ourselves, our communities, and our world as a whole. Upon closer inspection, it is clear that the shadow does not necessarily only contain those parts of us that are negative, but also good qualities that we have deemed inappropriate, unacceptable, or abnormal. Our shadow embodies our inner darkness, the parts of ourselves we wish to hide from the world and from our own minds, even the desires we have that we cannot satisfy.

It seems logical, then, to continue to suppress this self. If it is truly this volatile, this primal, this emotional, then it makes sense for us to separate it from the rest of ourselves.

However, this suppression serves only to further distance us from who we truly are, agitating our inner lives and creating a fundamental instability in our identities. The harder you fight against your shadow self and the deeper you try to hide it, the more difficult your relationship with that part of yourself will become. By refusing to accept this part of who you are, you continue to live your life, missing an integral part of what makes you *you*. You also can't give yourself wholly to the shadow self, allowing the deepest parts of yourself to control your life. The solution is seeking stability and reconciliation with our shadow selves.

Here is where we find Lilith. With her character as one who refuses to hide and her mystical depiction as a mirror of all women, Lilith becomes an almost archetypal figure of the shadow self for all women. She becomes a guide to facing our repressed rage, our denied independence, and our vilified sensuality. By embracing her story, we, by extension, embrace our own shadow selves, helping define us as people and not archetypes or vessels for male desire and dominance. Her story reflects the consequences of suppression by showing us what happens when men dictate how the lives of women are told; an empowering figure twisted into a warning for women. But there is also the power of reclamation as her story is embraced anew by women, turning from a shadowy demon to a shadowy beacon of hope and courage.

This highlights Lilith's role in integrating our shadows into ourselves. Through her defiance and authenticity, we can be inspired to acknowledge the feelings we've long repressed, face our fears of the unknown, and reclaim our suppressed strengths. Just like Lilith and self-exile, we will prioritize ourselves and our peace of mind over the expectations and demands of the world around us.

Throughout this process, you are likely to come face to face with parts of yourself that you did not wish to encounter. There are many aspects of your shadow self that might come to the surface, such as:

- Self-doubt

- Shame

- Unacknowledged anger

- Fear of rejection, failure, and even fear of success

- Self-sabotaging tendencies

- Compulsions and addictions

- Projecting unwanted traits or feelings to others

- Jealousy

- Codependency

- Seeking isolation

- Unexpressed desires

- Harsh self-judgement

- Perfectionism

- Guilt over your desires

These can be hard to discover and even harder to accept. But just like Lilith, you will find the strength within yourself to rise to the occasion, embrace the parts of you that have hidden all this time, and rise like the dark goddess to new heights.

Practices for Shadow Work with Lilith

You are not alone on this journey. There are many ways for you to engage in shadow work, remembering that Lilith is your guide and guardian in discovering your autonomy, rebellion, suppressed desires, and empowerment.

Journaling Prompts

- What emotions am I afraid to express? What would happen if I let them out?

- When do I feel anger or resentment? What is the source of these feelings?

- What desires do I keep secret, and why?

- What traits in women have I been taught to fear, reject, or criticize? Do I see these traits in myself?

- How do I feel about being seen as "too much" (e.g., too loud, too emotional, too sexual)?

- Where in my life am I giving my power away? How can I take it back?

- What do I feel most ashamed of? What would happen if I let go of that shame?

- How do I see Lilith within myself? What parts of her story resonate with me?

- When have I held back my truth because I feared judgment?

- How do I feel about being labeled as "difficult" or "rebellious"?

- How can I honor my shadow without letting it control me?

- If Lilith were to speak to me, what might she say about my struggles and desires?

- What does Lilith teach me about living unapologetically and embracing my whole self?

Meditations

Guided Visualization with Lilith:

1. Close your eyes and imagine yourself standing at the edge of a vast desert under a night sky. Feel the coolness of the air and hear the distant call of an owl.

2. In the distance, you see a figure illuminated by the moonlight. It is Lilith, standing tall and radiant. Her presence draws you forward.

3. Lilith welcomes you steadily and invites you to confront your truth.

4. Lilith asks you to look inward and call forth the parts of yourself that you've hidden. What do you see? How do these shadow aspects make you feel?

5. Lilith encourages you to speak with these shadows and listen to why these parts of you exist and what they have to teach

you. Lilith reminds you that these aspects are sources of power and wisdom.

6. Lilith places her hands over your heart and says: "*You are whole. You are powerful. You are free.*" Feel her energy infusing you with strength and self-acceptance.

7. Before you leave, Lilith offers you a gift. It could be an object, a word, or a feeling. Take this gift, knowing it represents your connection to your authentic self.

8. Lilith steps back into the shadows. Slowly, the desert fades, and you are back in your physical space. Wiggle your fingers and toes, take a deep breath, and open your eyes.

Releasing Shame Meditation:

1. Imagine roots growing from your body, anchoring you deep into the earth.

2. Remember a moment when you've experienced shame and note where this shame resides in your body. Without judgment, acknowledge its presence.

3. Imagine a warm light glowing in your heart, representing unconditional love and compassion. With each breath, this light grows brighter and warmer, expanding outwards.

4. Visualize the shame carried by the golden light. As you exhale, imagine it leaving your body, dissolving into the air, or being absorbed by the earth.

5. Repeat: "*I am worthy of love and acceptance. I release shame and embrace my true self. I forgive myself and honor my journey.*"

6. Visualize the golden light filling the spaces the shame had occupied, filling you with warmth, peace, and self-compassion.

7. Take a few deep breaths, grounding yourself back into the room, and when you're ready, open your eyes.

Rituals

Ritual for Embracing Anger:

1. Light a candle and take a few deep breaths, focusing on the flame.

2. Write down what you are angry about without judgment.

3. Read your words aloud, acknowledging your anger.

4. Say: "*I honor the anger as a teacher and source of strength. I release its hold on me.*"

5. Burn the paper in a fire-safe bowl. Imagine the fire transforming your rage into energy you can use positively.

6. As the paper burns, say: "*I channel my anger into power, clarity, and action. I am free.*"

7. Extinguish the candle and dispose of the ashes, symbolizing the release of your anger.

Full Moon Ritual:

1. Find an outdoor or window-lit space where you can see the moon. Light a candle and place a bowl of water nearby. Take a moment to connect with the moonlight and Lilith's energy.

2. Write down aspects of yourself you struggle to accept. Hold the paper and say: "*Lilith, guide me as I embrace my shadows and release what holds me back.*"

3. Tear the paper into pieces, placing them in the bowl of water. Visualize the moonlight dissolving these shadows.

4. Look at the moon and say: "*I honor my whole self—light and shadow. With Lilith's strength, I rise empowered.*"

5. Extinguish the candle and pour the water onto the earth, symbolizing your release and renewal. Thank Lilith and the moon for their guidance.

The Transformative Power of Embracing Lilith

Working with Lilith's unapologetic energy can empower you to accept yourself fully. Facing the shadow self leads to the emergence of liberation and creativity that cannot be overstated. Continuously reflect on the journey you're undertaking with Lilith so far: What parts of your shadow self have you begun to uncover? How do you honor all these parts of yourself?

Take the time to embrace self-acceptance and channel your shadows into personal growth. Transform the suppressed parts of you into empowerment. Let go of shame, anger, and fear, and reconnect with the autonomy that connects you to powerful women like Lilith.

Her steadfast refusal in the face of male domination and endurance in biased male depictions give women the strength to see Lilith as a role model for accepting the 'darker' parts of themselves. Together, we will find a way to balance our shadow selves in our daily lives, interacting with and overcoming them through self-reflection, meditation, and daydreaming. Like Lilith, we will discover ourselves all over again, rewrite our characters and stories, and achieve harmony with the things we have denied in ourselves. We will make peace with who we are, express our repressed desires in a healthy way, and heal the damage we have experienced from this world.

Remember, our 'shadows' make us who we are.

This healing will pave the way for confronting our unconscious and contribute to personal growth. Women are constantly bombarded by pressure to hide their "unacceptable" emotions, like anger, jealousy, or fear; these feelings are celebrated in men (think of the rage men exhibit when their favorite sports team doesn't win, or their envy towards other men with better bodies, more money, 'prettier girls' than them, or their emotional stuntedness). Emotions such as this are what make us who we are.

Of course, they must be regulated at times. Of course, we cannot let them dictate our lives. Of course, we cannot give in fully to how these emotions may push us to act if they harm ourselves and those around us.

But we must be allowed to *feel* them.

And now that you've glimpsed your shadow and begun to reclaim your inner power, how will you harness this energy to live your life?

Chapter 3

Lilith and Sexual Sovereignty

L ooking at Lilith's story, one can begin to wonder what it would feel like to embrace our sensuality unapologetically. What if women looked at our sexuality more than just something to be defined by, to be controlled by, to be shamed by? What if we saw it for what it truly is— a source of power, freedom, and joy?

Through Lilith, we find a symbol of sexual liberation, a figure who defied patriarchal constraints in order to boldly claim her autonomy and sexual desire. From the very inception of her character, she is a woman who embraces all that women are taught to hide and suppress about their sexuality. This is a battle all women are unfortunately deeply familiar with. Whether she is called a prude and a "bitch" for setting her boundaries, or a tease and a "slut" for embracing her sensual side, a woman is not permitted to be in control of her sexuality and desires.

When it comes to sexuality, women are only allowed to be tools of men in bed, existing and forming for their pleasure, regardless of their own wants and needs. A woman can be sexual only if a *man* wishes her to be. A woman can only exhibit sexual desire if it is within the context *men* have permitted. A woman can only dress however "modestly" or "provocatively" in terms of what *men* deem appropriate.

This is where the Dark Goddess and her feminine energy emerge to give us the courage and confidence to stand firm and understand our sensuality outside of the realm of men. We discover Lilith's role in challenging societal taboos, embracing sacred sexuality, and reclaiming the sexual sovereignty of women.

Lilith's Defiance of Patriarchal Norms

From the onset of Lilith's appearance in religious thought in the Jewish text of *The Alphabet of Ben Sira*, she stands as a symbol of sexual freedom. The crux of the story stems from her refusal to submit to Adam and lie under him, wishing to instead lie by his side as they were both created from the same earth. Adam's staunch refusal of this and his insistence on his own superiority was the revelation to Lilith that she could not be fully embraced and respected in Eden. It's important to remember that afterward, Lilith was not shunned from heaven, but in fact, left of her own volition, choosing self-exile over sexual submission to a man.

This was ultimately framed as one of the greatest crimes and sins a woman can commit, combining sexual liberation with disobedience. Subsequently, her story became warped and contorted by men who wished to use her as a warning to intimidate women into falling in line. This patriarchal backlash demonized her autonomy and painted her as a threat to societal norms, exposing that the patriarchal society viewed women's freedom as abnormal and inherently antithetical to society.

They did not stop at the oldest account of *The Alphabet* either; men, both religious and secular, throughout history invented tall tales regarding Lilith as a seductress and sexual fiend. She was portrayed as one who forced herself on Adam to spawn hundreds of demons, and that her spirit would sneak upon 'innocent' and unsuspecting men in their sleep to force herself on them. This narrative is one that is almost ironic and elicits an indignance in women at this reversal of the most common reality of female sexual oppression and violence.

Yes, women sexual abusers exist. However, associating a woman who simply demanded her equality with one who was abusive is a clear sign of the vilification of women's sexuality.

Throughout history, it has been women who have suffered from oppression of their sexuality, even in the most subtle of ways. Patriarchal systems have always sought to control and shame female sexuality and liberation. From the early modern period, where the majority of the tens of thousands who were executed for witchcraft were women, the patriarchy punished those who defied societal norms, lived independently or exhibited knowledge, usually healing and midwifery, that threatened the existing power structures. Lilith's story, especially later renditions, parallels the persecution of these women who refused to conform, encouraging us to invoke her energy to reclaim the power and wisdom women once risked their lives for. The witch becomes a figure of empowerment, not fear.

Afterward, as Lilith continued to be a figure demonized by men during the Romantic and then Victorian eras in literature and art, embracing her energy becomes more poignant. The Victorian era's strict 'moral codes' regulated women's behavior, restricted their autonomy in education, work, and personal expression, limited their knowledge of sexuality reinforced ideals of modesty, chastity, and submission to male authority. Women who deviated were seen as scandalous and immoral—Lilith championed those women who were ostracized by society for their rejection of subservience and obedience.

This continues into our modern times with the movements that promoted purity culture in the 1990s. Women were, and still are, idealized as "virginal" and "pure creatures" who must never exhibit behaviors outside sexual innocence, modesty, and submissiveness. Of course, Lilith's departure from Eden symbolizes the rejection of such imposed roles that stem from sexual control and not the protection they claim.

Ultimately, Lilith's energy inspires those seeking freedom from the shame tied to sexuality. Her narrative continues to resonate with contemporary movements like those encouraging sexual positivity and feminist empowerment. We have finally achieved a world where women are starting to reclaim their bodies, their desires, and their sexual expressions. There are now open discussions, both physically and online, about female pleasure and needs, with no shame attached. Many institutes and entities have launched campaigns promoting body positivity, highlighting the beauty of all female bodies, regardless of their diversity. Physical perfection is no longer the goal—women are embracing the "flaws" and "imperfections" that society pressured them to hide and accept their bodies' needs and wants.

There still persists a lingering culture of shaming sensuality, especially around female pleasure and desire. However, in the face of these oppressive norms, by reclaiming their sexuality, women empower and encourage self-expression. Sexuality and sensuality have never been something to be ashamed of. They are sacred, divine forces, energies that transform a person. That is what Lilith represents: a symbol of honoring the body, its desires, and the power of sexual expression.

Embracing sensuality is not merely about sexual acceptance. Through understanding the sanctity of sensuality, you acknowledge its healing power over you, helping heal your body from shame, past traumas, and feelings of being disconnected from yourself. Sexual sovereignty cannot be separated from your overall confidence in yourself and the self-love you feel.

Practices for Reclaiming Sexual Sovereignty

Reconnecting with our sensual selves can be a daunting task, particularly in a world that occasionally still villainizes women who wholeheartedly embrace their sexuality. Yet, through channeling Lilith's empowering energy, we invite you to reclaim the sexual sovereignty you were denied for so long.

Meditative Visualization

Lilith's Sanctuary:

1. Sit or lie in a comfortable position. Close your eyes and take several deep breaths.

2. Imagine yourself walking through a dense forest bathed in moonlight. You step forward into a hidden cave, lit by candles and crystals, smelling of earth and wildflowers.

3. At the center of this sacred sanctuary, Lilith waits for you. You sit beside her, her presence grounding you.

4. Lilith asks you to place your hands on your body, anywhere you feel. She whispers: "*Feel your body's wisdom. This vessel is sacred, strong, and deserving of love.*"

5. Lilith invites you to think of a desire you've suppressed. Imagine this desire as a flame growing in your chest.

6. Lilith places her hand over yours and says: "*You are worthy of love, freedom, and pleasure. Your body is yours, your desires are sacred, and your power is infinite.*"

7. Let her words sink into your body and become part of your being.

8. Hold this sense of worth and autonomy as you step out of the sanctuary into the moonlit forest, carrying Lilith's energy inside you.

Affirmations for Sexual Sovereignty

Using affirmations such as these regularly —whether you repeat them aloud, write them in a journal, or meditate on them— will help release you from society's conditioning.

- My body belongs to me, and I honor its wisdom and desires.

- I embrace my sexuality as a natural and beautiful part of who I am.

- I am free to explore and express my sexuality without fear or judgment.

- I trust my intuition to guide me in choosing what feels right for my body and soul.

- My desires are valid, and I honor them with curiosity and compassion.

- I am deserving of love, pleasure, and connection on my own terms.

- My body is sacred, and my pleasure is my birthright.

- I am free to define my sexuality on my own terms.

Rituals for Sensual Empowerment

Self-Love Ritual

1. Set up your quiet space, preferably near a mirror.

2. Arrange rose petals around a bowl of water or scatter them in your bathtub.

3. Light a candle, close your eyes, and take several deep breaths.

4. Whisper or speak aloud your intention for the ritual, whether you are celebrating your body or reclaiming your sensuality.

5. Gently place your hands on your heart and then on other parts of your body. With each touch, say an affirmation and thank your body for all it has given you.

6. Dip your hands into the bowl of water or step into your bath, feeling the rose petals on your skin.

7. Say: *"I release judgment and embrace my body's beauty and sensuality."*

8. Hold the candle and look into the mirror, repeating worthy affirmations to yourself.

9. Gently dry off and blow out the candle.

10. Reflect on how you can carry this sense of self-love into your daily life.

Full Moon Dance

1. Find an open space where you can move freely, ideally outdoors under the moonlight.

2. Wear comfortable clothes for ease of movement and remain barefoot to feel grounded.

3. Begin by standing still, feet planted firmly. Close your eyes and take deep breaths.

4. Then, start with small movements—sway your hips, roll your shoulders, stretch your arms.

5. Allow your movements to grow bigger and more expressive. Spin, jump, stomp, do whatever feels natural.

6. As you dance, focus on different parts of your body. Celebrate how they feel in their natural state.

7. When you feel ready to stop, gently slow your movements until you stand still with your hands to your heart or open to the sky.

8. Look up at the moon and say: *"Thank you for witnessing my freedom and guiding me to honor my body and spirit."*

These practices and guided meditations are ways in which we can embrace Lilith's energy. Not only does this serve to strengthen our sexual sovereignty, but it helps us build confidence and habits of self-love. Once you learn to accept that, like Lilith, your body is your own and there is no part of it that is not beautiful, your self-esteem grows. You see yourself as a person worth love and happiness. It nurtures a care inside you that cannot be achieved in any other way. And once you see yourself in such lights, it is almost impossible not to see that light in others as well. Embracing Lilith's energy can help you foster healthier and more authentic connections with others, especially women. When we realize we are all in the same boat, hidden goddesses alike, we can start to build on this sisterhood and empower one another. This will ultimately lead to challenging societal narratives about gender, sexuality, and control.

Integrate yourself with Lilith's energy. Outgrow the beliefs about your sexuality the world would instill in you. Honor your body and its desires as sacred. And take meaningful steps towards embracing your sexual sovereignty.

Because as you reclaim your sexuality, you reclaim your full self—wild, free, and divine.

Chapter 4

Lilith in Modern Feminism and Spirituality

What happens when an ancient symbol of defiance meets a world awakening to equality and empowerment?

In the modern world, Lilith has experienced a sort of rebirth in her new adoption as an important figure in feminist circles, popular culture, and even neo-pagan beliefs and spirituality. She is timeless, her story resonating deeply with modern movements that center around feminism, creativity, and spiritual liberation. That is no surprise. Given Lilith's determined presence in public consciousness and her refusal to adhere to societal expectations or norms, she becomes a role model and inspiration for others who share in this hope for a more liberated world.

Contemporary culture takes great influence from Lilith and her story, whether it's to reinterpret her story as one of feminist rage and equality, or emphasizing her demonic status but portraying it as a positive aspect. She has been the villain and the hero. A sublime goddess and a seductive devil. But maybe it is time to look at her as a woman—a woman who refused injustice, who took what she was owed, and who stood the test of time as a testament to strength and freedom. And *this* is the woman who has been adopted as a spiritual guide to achieving liberation within oneself.

Lilith as a Feminist Icon

Many women in the creative fields have taken it upon themselves to reimagine Lilith or be inspired by her story to create incredible depictions of the female soul. Whether in literature, poetry, art, or music, Lilith continues to be a symbol of rebellion against patriarchal constraints and a way to channel defiance and resilience. She has been evoked in poetry anthologies like Marge Piercy's *The Moon is Always Female* (1980) to celebrate female strength and individuality, fighting against those who vilify women who seek their freedom.

Even in art, Lilith continues to inspire women, as Kiki Smith sculpts a hauntingly lifelike depiction of her in 1994. In this version of the story, Lilith is crouched, staring upward, and her body is poised in defiance. By placing the sculpture on a wall instead of a pedestal, Smith symbolizes her separation from traditional societal roles, rejecting the "pure angel on the pedestal" role that many women are forced into.

As a demon and Queen of Hell, Lilith forges unforgettable characters in modern and contemporary stories and films. By appearing in Neil Gaiman's comic series, *The Sandman*, Cassandra Clare's *Shadowhunters* series, the TV shows *True Blood*, *Supernatural*, *Lucifer*, *Hazbin Hotel*, and many more, she is allowed versatility and a multi-faceted character, becoming more than just a monster, but a figure with depth, flaws, and strengths.

Music is also a medium that takes great inspiration from Lilith, embodied mainly in the 'Lilith Fair' —the all-female music festival, founded by Sarah McLachlan, in celebration of women's creativity and strength in an industry often dominated by men. Individual singers who are known to champion female strength and feminist ideals also make constant reference to Lilith. For example, the American singer Halsey, in her album *If I Can't Have Love, I Want Power*, has a track titled "Lilith," in which she addresses many feminist themes, denouncing the idea that women are inherently hostile or villainous and that they are complex human beings with desire and ambition.

Even in feminist movements and campaigns, Lilith is embraced as a symbol of resistance, resilience, and reclamation of agency. Her energy is continuously invoked to encourage unapologetic self-expression in women who wish to challenge gender inequality. In movements regarding sex-positive feminism, Lilith's embrace of her sexuality becomes a symbol of liberation, with activists invoking her in campaigns against purity culture and slut-shaming. Movements like *#MeToo* reflect her energy in their efforts to dismantle systems that police women's bodies, and her story inspires survivors to reclaim their narratives.

Other campaigns that carry Lilith's energy include the discourse around reproductive rights. Lilith's autonomy over her body becomes a symbol to fight legislation that restricts women's bodily autonomy, highlighting their right to choose, *#MyBodyMyChoice*. Echoing Lilith's defiance and her connection to early depictions of witches and demonesses, the *#WitchTheVote* campaign harnessed her rebellion to encourage women to vote and reclaim their political power. More hashtags like *#LilithRising* also highlight stories of empowerment and resistance, particularly with marginalized voices reclaiming their narratives. Women are holding workshops centered around Lilith's archetype that encourage others to connect with their inner power, reject societal norms, and embrace their unique identities. All of this is done in Lilith's name and through her energy.

Neo-Paganism and Goddess-Centered Spirituality

Delving deeper into connections with spirituality, in many neo-pagan and goddess-centered practices, Lilith is revered as an archetype of fierce independence and sacred sexuality. Throughout history and in certain religious circles, Lilith was demonized for the traits she exhibited, and these practitioners aim to turn her from a figure of fear to one of exaltation. Women-led groups carry out rituals to invoke her energy and honor the resilience of those who resist oppression. Within these practices, she becomes associated with ancient, powerful goddesses like Diana, the Roman goddess of the Moon, the hunt, wildlife, and childbirth. She joins the neo-pagan religious movement of the Goddess, being worshipped alongside such counterparts as the Mesopotamian Inanna, the Ancient Egyptian Isis, the Greek Aphrodite, and the Hindu Sarasvati. Here, the female deity is the primary, and like Lilith, derives her power equally to men.

Regarding Lilith, her dual nature as both a nurturing spirit that protects women and an untamed spirit of the wild embodies the complexities of the divine feminine. Similar to other pagan goddesses, like the Hellenistic Persephone, who was both Queen of the Underworld and Goddess of Spring, nature could not be attributed to a single image. In these beliefs, people, and especially women, should not let society demarcate them into clear and limited boxes. Modern spiritual practitioners invoke Lilith's energy to confront their fears, harness their autonomy, and reclaim their inner power. As previously seen in this book, Lilith has a deep connection to themes like empowerment, shadow work, and healing from patriarchal conditioning, all of which work on bringing your spirit closer to the Dark Goddess.

Practices for Invoking Lilith's Energy

We can take inspiration from the practitioners of neo-paganism and goddess-centered spirituality to find methods and rituals to bring us closer to Lilith and channel her energy in a healthy and positive way.

Rituals to Connect with Lilith

Invocation Ritual:

1. Cleanse your space with incense or whatever your preferred method is.

2. Place a candle at the center of your sacred space and arrange an offering (e.g., wine, dark chocolate, or flowers) beside it. Light the candle.

3. Sit and close your eyes. Take several deep breaths, feeling grounded in the earth.

4. Present your offering to Lilith and invite her presence and guidance into your sacred space.

5. Chant and repeat as many times as feels natural the following:

   "Lilith, keeper of wisdom and fire,

   Guide me to my truest desire.

   Shadow mother, fierce and free,

   I honor your power within me."

6. Visualize Lilith's presence and imagine her standing before you, offering strength and guidance.

7. Speak your affirmations to embody Lilith's energy: "*I embrace my shadow and my light. I claim my desires without fear or shame. I am free, powerful, and whole.*"

8. Thank Lilith for her presence and extinguish the candle, keeping her energy within you.

Altar Setups

Remember that your alter setup is a living, evolving space. Through it, you gain a powerful tool for reflection and transformation.

- **Elements of the Altar:**

    o Black candles for protection and shadow work.

    o Red candles for passion, vitality, and courage.

    o Red roses, or dried petals, for desire and self-love.

    o Serpentine crystals for transformation.

    o Obsidian crystals for grounding and protection.

    o Carnelian crystals for channeling creativity and sensuality.

o   Owl symbols for wisdom and Lilith's nocturnal nature (can be small statuettes, illustrations, or feathers).

o   Serpent symbols for rebirth and knowledge (jewelry, figurines, or art).

o   Moon symbols for feminine power and the subconscious.

o   Offerings like dark chocolate, red wine, pomegranate seeds, or incense (myrrh, frankincense, or dragon's blood)

o   Personal items that hold meaning to you, like jewelry, trinkets, journals, or tarot cards.

Connect with and use your altar to extract the benefits from harnessing Lilith's energy. Engage in daily rituals where you light a candle and meditate, reciting affirmations or journaling at the altar to focus on Lilith's guidance in your life. With each passing season, refresh your altar with flowers and symbols that align with the natural cycles, deepening your connection to Lilith. There are no strict rules or limitations here. As long as you approach your altar with respect and purpose, you may use it as a space for rituals, shadow work, or any quiet reflection you need to connect with your inner self.

Guided Meditations

Empowerment Meditation:

1. Light a candle and sit or lie down in a relaxed position, closing your eyes and taking a few deep breaths.

2. Imagine roots growing from your body into the earth and, with each inhale, draw in energy from the earth, and with each exhale, release any fear or tension.

3. Visualize a red or black light representing Lilith's presence glowing above you. Imagine this light filling your body and connecting you to Lilith's defiant, untamed spirit.

4. Repeat your affirmations: *"I release fear and embrace my power." "I honor my autonomy and boundaries."*

5. Visualize a moment when you felt powerless and imagine Lilith standing beside you in support. See yourself reclaiming your voice and your power in that moment.

6. Picture yourself standing tall, a shield of light surrounding you, protecting you from harm. You are untamed, unapologetic, and unimpeded.

7. Extinguish the candle, continuing to carry Lilith's strength within you.

Lilith's story continues to be an inspiration for contemporary empowerment. From myth to modern movement, Lilith bridges ancient mythology with today's quest for equality, self-realization, and authenticity. Through her story, we are inspired to confront societal and personal limitations, awakening to our true selves. Connecting with her as a guide carries with it a transformative power that leads to deeper self-awareness and growth. As we've seen, there are many ways to honor and channel her energy in our daily lives, as she remains relevant to our personal and spiritual journeys.

As you connect with Lilith's fierce yet protective energy, you step into your power and become part of a legacy of defiance and strength.

Chapter 5

Living with Lilith's Energy

We've seen the energy Lilith invokes in psychology, sexuality, popular culture, literature, art, music, feminist movements, and neo-pagan spirituality. But those are all grand narratives, major instances in life and the world where women can embody Lilith and take a stand against the overarching structures that oppress and limit their power. But what about the day-to-day experience of women? What about women who do not wish to create huge world-changing and life-altering events every day of their lives?

That is why we ask these women, what if you could carry Lilith's fearless energy with you in every decision, every relationship, every moment of your self-expression?

Our connection with Lilith does not need to be earth-shattering. Lilith's transformative energy can find its way into our daily living with methods of integrating the ideals she stood for in the minutiae of everyday existence. We need to remember that Lilith is not only the goddess of rebellion but also a guide to living authentically and fearlessly.

Lessons from Lilith for Everyday Life

When we go back to Lilith's story with Adam, we see that she teaches us much about balancing independence with our relationships, whether they are romantic, familial, or platonic. In almost all iterations, Lilith never *refused* to be Adam's wife or rejected the notion of partnership and companionship; she merely asserted that should they be partners, they would be on equal footing. The lesson she inspires through her assertion of her autonomy is that she was still attempting to maintain a meaningful connection that was rejected by the other party. She stood her ground and claimed her right, which was to form a relationship on her own terms. Everyone should have the freedom and control in their lives to be able to set boundaries in any relationship without compromising the intimacy or mutual respect found. Later, we will explore healthy strategies to set boundaries for yourself and the people you are connecting with.

As we've seen, the figure of Lilith has gone through many changes, with each society, particularly the patriarchy, fitting her in their mold of either a warning or a threat of what happens when a woman does not conform. We all experience this pressure to navigate our societal expectations and how we should think, speak, and behave. Lilith's refusal to conform, rejecting the offer from the angels sent by God, and embracing the dark aspects of herself all inspire women to follow in her footsteps and challenge the norms that limit their authenticity. It is not easy to do this; in a world that often rewards conformity, it takes true courage to live your truth and not follow the status quo.

Once this authenticity is unlocked inside us, it becomes easier to achieve self-expression and creativity. When you are free from the shackles society places on you, you have the opportunity to embrace your unique voice and explore your talents in your professional and personal lives. You can discover things about yourself that you never thought possible and unapologetically show them to the world. When each person unlocks new avenues of their selves, Lilith's energy becomes a catalyst for fostering innovation, breaking barriers, and inspiring change. Whether in your art, work, or simple problem-solving, harnessing her rebellious spirit will spark new and creative ways to approach any aspect of your life. Embodying her energy can help you overcome whatever fears are holding you back and, thus, allow you to step into your full potential. She is our mentor, leading us to the path of continual growth and self-discovery.

Practical Guidance for Living with Lilith's Energy

Affirmations for Empowerment

These are suggested affirmations that you can repeat out loud, write down, or incorporate into your regular rituals and meditations to channel empowerment.

- I am fearless in expressing my truth.

- I honor my boundaries as sacred.

- I am free to live my life without fear or apology.

- I release the need for external validation

- I embrace my shadow and my light, knowing both make me whole.

- I reclaim my power from all who tried to diminish it.

- I honor my worth and demand nothing less than respect.

- I am a reflection of Lilith's resilience and wisdom.

Boundary-Setting Exercises

- Clarify your boundaries by clearly identifying what behaviors, actions, or situations you allow in your life, the ones you don't allow or make you uncomfortable, and note what you need from yourself and others to feel secure and respected.

- Trust your instincts and hone them. Think of a situation where you're not sure about your boundaries. Imagine saying "Yes" and note how your body responds. Then, say "No" and see if your body feels more at ease. Use these physical cues to guide your boundary-setting.

- Work on creating boundary scripts by writing down common scenarios where your boundaries are challenged and reciting your script to assert your boundary. Practice these scripts out loud with a friend to feel more confident using them in real situations.

- Visualize a strong yet flexible boundary shield surrounding your body that allows love and positivity in but blocks out harmful energy and behaviors.

Mindfulness Practices

Many of the practical guidelines and meditations we've included here are great ways to promote mindfulness in all your actions and generally in how you live your life. From meditations that inspire you to visualize Lilith, meeting her in a dense forest or a sacred cave in the moonlight, and taking her gifts and reassurances, you can constantly practice embodying Lilith's strength and poise during challenging situations.

Sometimes, simple practices and rituals, such as lighting a candle or reciting affirmations, can set the tone for a day aligned with Lilith's energy. You can even practice awakening your senses and embracing your present moment, whatever it may be. Here's how you can do this:

1. Choose a small object with texture, smell, or taste that resonates with Lilith's energy (this could be a rose petal, a piece of dark chocolate, etc.).

2. Hold it in your hand and explore it with curiosity, asking: *"What does it feel like? Smell like? Taste like?"*

3. Let this deep focus bring you into the present moment, saying your affirmations: *"I deserve to savor life fully."*

To live aligned with our true essence is to live free from fear and limitation. An untethered liberation comes from releasing societal or self-imposed constraints and simply *being*. Lilith is more than just one part of feminine energy or dark goddess; she is complex and versatile, giving us the chance to embody her energy in all areas of life. Whether through fostering equal partnerships rooted in respect and authenticity, using Lilith's rebellious spirit to innovate and lead boldly, or honoring Lilith as a constant source of guidance and empowerment, she is with you every step of the way.

Lilith's energy is already within you—wild, bold, and unshakably real. Live it, embody it, and inspire others to do the same.

Conclusion

We have come to the end of our journey through Lilith's Energy and awakening the Lilith within each of us. We have explored, understood, and embodied the Dark Goddess as a symbol of divine feminine power and rebellion. We have gone deep into the earth and uncovered Lilith's mythological roots in Ancient Mesopotamia, Babylon, and Jewish traditions, then followed her evolution through history from a demoness to a seductive siren and ultimately to a protector of women. Through Carl Jung's ideas of the shadow self, we witnessed Lilith as the shadow of many women, representing the suppressed parts of our psyche and how we can and must learn to come to terms with her. She shone through as a beacon of sexual sovereignty to represent the form of empowerment and liberation that comes from rejecting patriarchal notions of purity and shame. Her influence on modern femininity and spirituality became paramount as Lilith formed the bridge connecting ancient wisdom to contemporary life. Finally, we understood what it took to live with her energy and to cultivate authenticity, resilience, and transformative power.

Lilith will always remain a guide for personal and collective transformation. Through her refusal to wither in the face of injustice, we can draw from her energy to stand our truths and challenge the limitations the world enforces on us. This is not an individual story. This is a birthright. And her story will continue to resonate across the collective consciousness, inspiring broader societal shifts toward gender equality and the celebration of diversity. Here is where we all embody her and become the rebellious spirit and agents of change in our own communities.

Lilith is timeless. Her message will endure across cultures, spiritual practices, and personal growth journeys. She is a reminder that the path to empowerment often requires embracing discomfort, defying norms, and reclaiming suppressed aspects of the self. She is a bridge between our past and our future, uniting ancient wisdom with the needs of a rapidly evolving world.

Do not stop your journey here. Deepen your connection with Lilith beyond this book and set intentions for ongoing transformation. Continue integrating Lilith-inspired affirmations, meditations, and creative expressions in your daily life, and even consider joining feminist or spiritual groups, workshops, or online spaces that align with your newfound self-actualization.

Do not see Lilith as an external figure, far away and distant; instead, picture her as an energy that is already present within you.

Think about what she has awakened in you throughout this journey and how you can honor her for it. Read more, express yourself in whatever way feels right to you, and practice the spirituality that Lilith's legacy has inspired.

Lilith's story is yours now. You are bold, unapologetic, and fiercely free. The journey has only just begun.

References

Beaucham, C. (2009). Lilith and Mysticism. *North Wind: A Journal of George MacDonald Studies, 28*(1), 2.

Bibi, N. (2024). The Shadow Self: An Investigation into unconscious aspects of personality and their manifestations in Behavior. *Jahan-e-Tahqeeq, 7*(1), 430-447.

Braun, S. D. (1982). Lilith: Her Literary Portrait, Symbolism, and Significance. *Nineteenth-Century French Studies, 11*(1/2), 135-153.

Dame, E., Rivlin, L., & Wenkart, H. (Eds.). (1998). *Which Lilith?: Feminist Writers Re-Create the World's First Woman.* Jason Aronson, Incorporated.

Dion, N. M. (2006). Worshipping the dark: the manifestations of Carl Gustav Jung's archetype of the shadow in contemporary Wicca.

Hoy, E. (2012). How do shifting depictions of Lilith,'The First Eve', trace the contexts and hegemonic values of their times?. *Teaching History, 46*(3), 54-59.

Hurwitz, S. (1999). *Lilith-the first eve: Historical and psychological aspects of the dark feminine.* Daimon.

Kristeller, J. (2011). Spirituality and meditation. https://psycnet.apa.org/record/2010-19903-008

Landau, R. (2024). The Dark Feminine Rising: A Psychocultural and Clinical Meditation. In *Jungian Analysis in a World on Fire* (pp. 58-75). Routledge.

LeVine, K. (2020). Reclaiming Lilith as a Strong Female Role Model. https://digitalcommons.linfield.edu/relsstud_theses/5/

McDonald, B. E. (2009). In possession of the night: Lilith as goddess, demon, vampire. In *Sacred Tropes: Tanakh, New Testament, and Qur'an as Literature and Culture* (pp. 173-182). Brill.

Perry, C., & Tower, R. (Eds.). (2023). *Jung's Shadow Concept: The Hidden Light and Darkness Within Ourselves*. Taylor & Francis.

Petchsawang, P., & McLean, G. N. (2017). Workplace spirituality, mindfulness meditation, and work engagement. *Journal of Management, Spirituality & Religion, 14*(3), 216-244.

Plaskow, J. (2015). *The Coming of Lilith: Essays on Feminism, Judaism, and Sexual Ethics, 1972-2003*. Beacon Press.

Ruah–Midbar Shapiro, M. (2019). Lilith's Comeback from a Jungian-Feminist Outlook: Contemporary Feminist Spirituality Gets into Bed with Lilith. *Feminist theology, 27*(2), 149-163.

Ruah-Midbar Shapiro, M. (2019). The temptation of legitimacy: Lilith's adoption and adaption in contemporary feminist spirituality and their meanings. *Modern Judaism-A Journal of Jewish Ideas and Experience, 39*(2), 125-143.

Schaeffer, B. (2023). *The History and Transcendence of Lilith: Understanding the Ancient Myth and Exploring Its Recent Use in the Feminist Movement* (Master's thesis, Idaho State University).

Smith, T. L. (2008). *Lilith: a mythological study* (Doctoral dissertation, University of Bedfordshire).

Von Stuckrad, K. (1999). *Constructing Femininity: The Lilith Case.* LAUD.

Williamson, J. (2020). The Evolution of Lilith: The World's First Feminist. *Evolution.*